How Things Grow

From Tadpole

to Frog

Sally Morgan

Belitha Press

First published in the UK in 2002 by
(✦) Belitha Press
A member of **Chrysalis** Books plc
64 Brewery Road, London N7 9NT

Copyright © Belitha Press Ltd 2002
Text by Sally Morgan

ISBN 1 84138 374 0

British Library Cataloguing in Publication Data
for this book is available from the British Library.

Series editor: Jean Coppendale
Designer: Angie Allison
Picture researchers: Sally Morgan and Terry Forshaw
Consultant: Bethan Currenti

Printed in Hong Kong

10 9 8 7 6 5 4 3 2 1

Picture acknowledgements:
All photography Chrysalis Images/Robert Pickett with the exception of:
6 & 30, 7 (T) & 28 (BL) Papilio; 7 (B) Ecoscene/Anthony Cooper; 8 & front cover (inset),
10 & 28 (TL & TR) Papilio; 13 (T) Ecoscene/Neil Miller; 19 NHPA/Nigel J. Dennis; 20
Oxford Scientific Films/Paulo De Oliveira; 22, front cover (inset) & 28 (BR) Ecoscene/
Ian Beames; 25 Papilio; 26 & back cover (R) Ecoscene/Robin Redfern; 27 Papilio.

Contents

What is a frog? 4

Laying eggs 6

Inside a frog's egg 8

From egg to tadpole 10

Tadpoles 12

Two legs 14

Four legs 16

Leaving the pond 18

Hunting 20

Surviving winter 22

Getting old 24

The frog family 26

The life cycle 28

Glossary 30

Index 32

What is a frog?

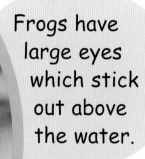

Frogs have large eyes which stick out above the water.

A frog is a small animal with four legs. It has strong back legs that are great for jumping and swimming. Frogs have a slightly wet skin, which dries out easily. They live in wet places on land.

Once a year, frogs find a pond where they can **breed**. The female frog lays eggs which **hatch** into **tadpoles**. The tadpoles have to change their body shape to become a frog. This is called **metamorphosis** (meta-more-fo-sis).

The frog uses its long back legs to push through the water.

Laying eggs

In spring, frogs come out of their winter hiding places. They make their way to a pond. Lots of frogs gather in the pond. The male frogs are very noisy, especially at night.

A male frog puffs out a **pouch** on each side of its throat to make its croaks louder.

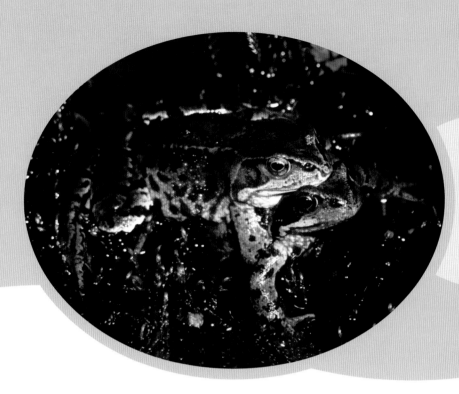

The male frog holds on to the female frog while she lays her eggs.

Each male **croaks** loudly to call to a female frog. The female frog is full of eggs. She lays about 100 eggs, which stick together in a clump. The egg clumps are called **frogspawn**.

Once the eggs have been laid, the frog leaves them to grow into tadpoles.

Inside a frog's egg

At first, a frog's egg is a tiny
black dot in the middle of a blob of jelly.
The black dot will grow into a new tadpole.
The clumps of frogspawn
float on the surface
of the pond.

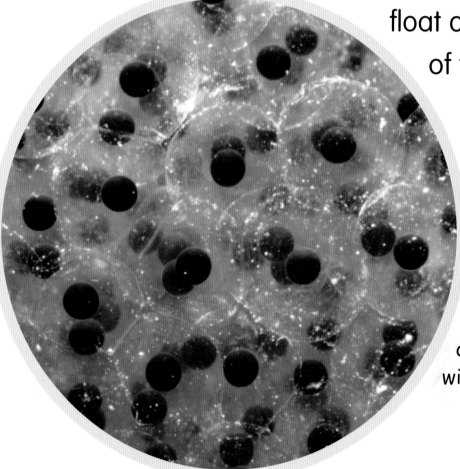

All the eggs
stick together
but not all
of them
will hatch .

The frogspawn may stick
to plants in the water. This
stops it from floating away.

The jelly slowly takes
up water and swells in size.
The jelly is very slippery. This
makes it difficult for animals
to eat the eggs.

From egg to tadpole

The black dot in the middle of the egg starts to grow larger and longer. Soon you can see a small head and tail. The dot has become a tadpole.

After a few days, the black dot begins to look like a tiny tadpole.

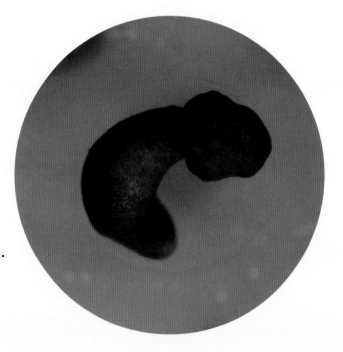

After ten days, the tadpole wriggles out of the jelly. At first, the tadpole stays close to the jelly or clings to pondweed. It does not need to eat for several days.

These tadpoles have just hatched. They don't look like frogs at all.

Tadpoles

The young tadpole has feathery **gills** on each side of its head. It uses the gills to breathe underwater.

The tadpole is a **herbivore**, which means that it eats plants. It feeds on **algae** in the water.

This tadpole has long feathery gills and a very long tail.

Newly hatched tadpoles cling to the jelly because they are weak and cannot swim very far.

The tadpole stays
in the **shallow** water, which
is warmer than the rest of the pond.
Now the tadpole begins to change
into a frog.

The tadpole is four weeks old. Now it breathes with new gills that have grown inside its body.

13

Two legs

When the tadpole is about eight weeks old, it starts to grow legs. Two tiny bumps appear at the back of its body. The bumps grow into legs.

The back legs appear at the back of the body, on either side of the tail.

The legs are small at first, but they soon become longer and thicker. Each leg ends in a **webbed foot**.

The tadpole eats plants such as duckweed. It also begins to eat tiny animals in the water.

The back legs grow larger and more powerful.

Four legs

The tadpole grows front legs a few weeks after the back legs. Its body changes shape. Its tail becomes shorter until there is only a short **stump**.

This tadpole swims to the surface of the water to take its first gulp of air.

There are also changes inside the tadpole's body. The tadpole grows **lungs**. Now it has to swim to the surface of the water to breathe air.

The tail of this tadpole has almost disappeared.

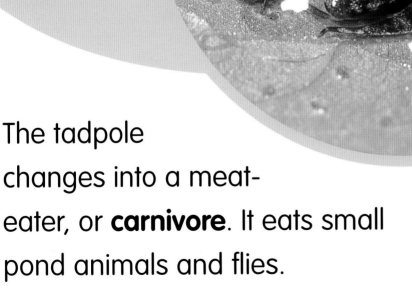

The tadpole changes into a meat-eater, or **carnivore**. It eats small pond animals and flies.

17

Leaving the pond

This
tiny frog is
ready to leave
the pond.

By early
summer,
the tadpole
has become a
tiny frog. It is about the
size of a fingernail.

The frog spends more time at the edge of the pond. It hides under stones and lily leaves. Finally, the frog climbs out of the water and starts its life on land.

Herons like to eat frogs and fish.

This is a dangerous time for the young frog. Many frogs are eaten by birds and other animals.

Hunting

The young frog eats flies and other small animals. Its eyes are good at spotting flies when they move. When the frog sees a fly, it shoots out its long tongue. The fly is trapped on the sticky tongue.

The frog has a long, sticky tongue to catch insects.

The frog has large feet which are like flippers. They push the frog through the water.

A frog can hop, jump, crawl and swim. It uses its long back legs to push its body forwards very quickly.

21

Surviving winter

The young frog grows quickly. By the end of the summer it is many times bigger than when it left the pond. The frog has to find a safe place where it can sleep through the cold winter.

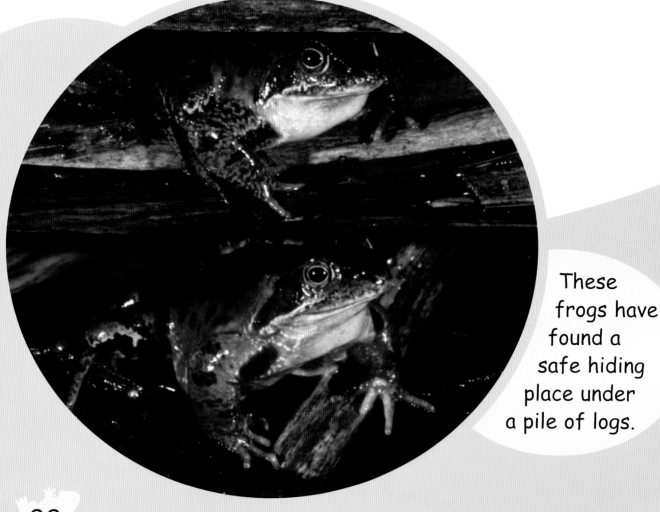

These frogs have found a safe hiding place under a pile of logs.

In spring
the days
become longer
and warmer. The
frog goes back
to its pond.

The best places for frogs to sleep are
under logs or in holes in the ground. The
frog stays in its hiding place until spring
arrives. Then it wakes up and travels
back to the pond where it was born.

Getting old

Pet frogs can live for 25 years
or more. Frogs in the wild do
not live for more than a few years.
Many frogs are eaten by animals

such as herons, foxes
and snakes.

This old frog
lives in a garden
pond. It is several
years old.

Many frogs are eaten by snakes.

Some frogs die from **disease** and others are squashed on the roads by cars. Frogs need ponds to **survive**. If a pond disappears, the frogs may die or have to move away.

The frog family

A toad is fatter than a frog, and its legs are shorter. It crawls rather than jumps.

Frogs belong to a group of animals called **amphibians** (am-fib-ians). Amphibians are animals that can live both in water and on land. But they have to return to water to lay their eggs.

Toads and newts are also amphibians. A toad looks a bit like a frog, but it has a dry and lumpy skin. A newt looks like a lizard. It has a long body and tail, with four short legs.

The tail of a newt is almost as long as its body. It leaves the water to hunt for slugs and worms on land.

The life cycle

1 A newly laid frog's egg is a tiny black dot in clear jelly.

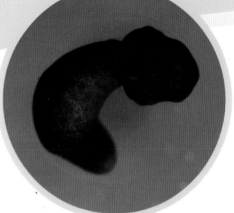

2 The black dot grows longer. It begins to look like a tiny tadpole.

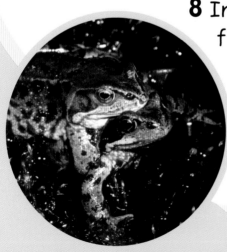

8 In spring, the frog makes its way back to a pond to find a **mate** and lay eggs.

7 The frog spends the winter months asleep under logs.

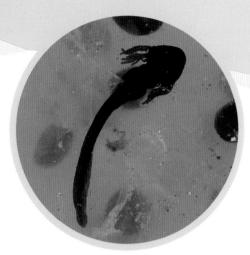

3 The tadpole grows gills. It is ready to wriggle out of the jelly.

4 The tadpole loses its feathery gills. It feeds on algae and pondweed in the water.

6 The tadpole's tail starts to shrink. Soon the tiny frog will be ready to leave the pond.

5 The tadpole's back legs grow. Then the front legs appear. The tadpole starts to breathe air.

Glossary

algae   Tiny plants that grow in water. They do not have leaves, stems or roots.

amphibians (am-fib-ians)   Animals that live in water and on land. Frogs, toads and newts are amphibians.

breed   To produce young.

carnivore   An animal that eats meat.

croaks   The name given to the sounds made by a frog.

disease   A serious illness.

frogspawn   The name given to the clump of eggs laid by a frog.

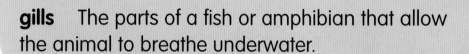

gills   The parts of a fish or amphibian that allow the animal to breathe underwater.

hatch   To come out of an egg.

herbivore   An animal that eats only plants.

lungs   Spongy structures that take in air when an animal breathes.

mate   To breed or pair in order to produce young.

mate The partner of an animal.

metamorphosis (meta-more-fo-sis) A change in body shape or appearance, as when a tadpole changes into an adult.

pouch Something shaped like a bag.

shallow Water that is not deep.

stump   The remains of something, for example the remains of a tadpole's tail.

survive To go on living, to stay alive.

tadpoles   The young form of a frog or toad, before they change into adults.

webbed foot A foot on which the toes are joined by pieces of skin.

index

algae 12, 30
amphibians 26–7, 30

breathing 12, 17
breed 5, 30

carnivores 17, 30
croaks 6, 7, 30

disease 25, 30

eggs 6–11, 26

feet 21
flies 20
food 15, 20
frog family 26–7
frogs 4–5

leaving pond 18–19

frogspawn 7, 8–9, 30

gills 12, 13, 30

hatch 5, 11, 30
herbivores 12, 30
hiding places 22–3
hunting 20–1

legs 4, 5, 14–17, 27
life cycle 28–9
lungs 17, 30

males 6–7
mate 31
metamorphosis 5, 31

skin 4, 27
spring 6–7, 23
swimming 4

tadpoles 5, 10–17, 31
tail 12, 16, 17, 27
toads 26, 27

webbed feet 15, 31
winter 22–3